FOR THE FATHER WHO HAS EVERYTHING

A Funny Book for Fathers

TeamGolfwell

For the Father Who Has Everything by Team Golfwell

FOR THE FATHER WHO HAS EVERYTHING, A Funny Book for Fathers, Copyright © 2022, Pacific Trust Holdings NZ Ltd. All rights reserved for the collective work only. No part of this book may be reproduced or transmitted in any form or by any means, electronic or mechanical, including photocopying, recording, or by any information storage and retrieval system, without written permission from the author, except for brief quotations as would be used in a review.

This is the third book in the series, *For Someone Who Has Everything.*

Cover by Design King. All images are from Creative Commons or Shutterstock

ISBN 9798411262834 (Amazon paperback)

ISBN 9781991156594 (Ingram Spark)

For the Father Who Has Everything by Team Golfwell

Who needs who the most? "When my daughter says, 'Daddy I need you!' I wonder if she has any idea that I need her billion times more."

— Stanley Behrman, Longtime writer for The New Yorker

Make your life easier. "I gave my father $100 and said, 'Buy yourself something that will make your life easier.' So, he went out and bought a present for my mother."

-- Rita Rudner

"Always knew that…"
"Daddy," I whispered, feeling my own breath hitch in my throat. "I love you."

Just when I was sure he was asleep, one corner of his mouth lifted in a smile.

"I knew that" he murmured. "Always knew that…"

— Morgan Matson, "Second Chance Summer"

Raising children. "Before I got married, I had six theories about raising children. Now, I have six children and no theories."

— John Wilmot (1647-1680) English Poet

"Watch your ass." "When I was 18, I thought I was in love. First time -- you know that magic feeling. So, I asked my father. I said, 'Dad is love real?'

"And he said, 'No. But herpes is, so watch your ass.'"

- Greg Fitzsimmons, Comedian

Best friend. "Dad is my best friend and is the only one that walks into your life when the world has walked out."

— Shannon Alder

Father suddenly becomes a genius. "When I was 17, my father was so stupid, I didn't want to be seen with him in public.

When I was 24, I was amazed at how much the old man had learned in just 7 years."

-- Mark Twain

A daughter's gift – I think? "My daughter got me a 'World's Best Dad' mug. So, we know she's sarcastic."

– Bob Odenkirk, Actor, comedian, writer, director

Try. "My father used to say that it's never too late to do anything you wanted to do. And he said, 'You never know what you can accomplish until you try.'"

— Michael Jordan

"I've lost my dad" Five-year-old Little Johnny was lost, so he went up to a policeman and said, "I've lost my dad!"

The policeman said, "What's he like?"

Little Johnny replied, "Beer and women!"

Bring her home on time. "I threw a shotgun shell at my daughter's date and told him it goes much faster after 10 pm."

– Anon.

Hide and seek. "I was watching kids play hide and seek in the yard and mine just hid behind a chain-link fence… Well at least I don't have to save for college."

– Unknown

"Give a dad a fish and he will eat it. Teach a dad to fish and he will drink beer on the dock."

– Unknown

What's a perfect dad? Children were asked this question. These are a few excerpts,

- An 11-year-old replied, "This is mine: a dad who drives you everywhere, cheers you on and loves you unconditionally. He listens to whatever I need to say, even if it is the craziest thing ever. If I need something, he will try his best to get it to me. He plays with our dog like he is a human. And whenever I am sad, he loves me."

- A 9-year-old replied, "My dad is the best because he makes me believe in myself. There was a talent show in my school. I was shy. He said, 'Don't give up — it's your dream.' When I heard him say that I knew it was time to shine, and I won the show!"

- An older child said, "I'll never forget the man who put me to sleep when I was having a bad day, who worked nonstop to see me to where I am now and who waited for me to continue my path through the future. The man that made me laugh and took me on the ride of my life, and who never expected less of me, only more."

- Another older child said, "When my parents got divorced, it was really tough grasping the fact that I will only be able to see my favorite person in the whole world over the weekends. At age 6, I learned his cell number by heart. It was the only one I knew. Nothing will ever break us apart."

- A 10-year-old replied, "My daddy inspires me to do my best at everything. Whenever I leave for school, we do our handshake and he tells me, 'Do great things.' He also inspires me because he was able to achieve his goal of being an architect. He makes me laugh by doing funny dances, making funny faces, and making funny noises. I especially laugh when he throws a grape in the air and catches it in his mouth."

Confident and Confidential.

Son: "Dad, what's the difference between confident and confidential?"

Dad: "Hmm. You are my son. Of that I am confident. Your friend Timmy is also my son. That's confidential."

You want a piece of me? Wrestling and roughhousing with dad help children to manage emotions and develop balance between thinking and physical action. "Perhaps out of worry for their kids' future financial security, dads across human cultures mostly focus on preparing children to compete within society. They give advice, encourage academic success and stress achievement," according to David Geary of the University of Missouri. [1]

By roughhousing, dads "rile them up, almost to the point that they are going to snap, and then calms them down," explains Geary. "This pattern teaches kids to control their emotions—a trait that garners them popularity among superiors and peers," he said. "As adults, they are more likely to form secure relationships, achieve stable social standing and become able parents.

"Also, in this sense, a father who takes care of his children also gives his grandchildren a leg up." [2]

Wrong answer! Last evening, I met my daughter's boyfriend for the first time, and I asked him what he does? …he's not going to be walking right for a while or be around since "Your daughter" wasn't the right answer.

Son runs into dad's ghost in a video game. Losing your dad at just six years of age is very tough, of course. Per Yahoo News, Motoramic, reports that a gamer who lost his father when he was six years old encountered him again (10 years later) in a video game they used to play together before the dad died. [3]

The game, "RalliSport Challenge" allowed players to save their best lap time as "ghosts" against which other players could race. Ten years after his father's death, the son decided to have another look at the game. This is the son's story,

"Well, when i was 4, my dad bought a trusty Xbox. you know, the first, ruggedy, blocky one from 2001.

we had tons and tons and tons of fun playing all kinds of games together - until he died, when i was just 6.

i couldn't touch that console for 10 years.

but once i did, i noticed something.

we used to play a racing game, Rally Sports Challenge. actually, pretty awesome for the time it came.

and once i started meddling around... i found a GHOST.

literally.

you know, when a time race happens, that the fastest lap so far gets recorded as a ghost driver? yep, you guessed it - his ghost still rolls around the track today.

and so, i played and played, and played, until i was almost able to beat the ghost. until one day i got ahead of it, i surpassed it, and...

i stopped right in front of the finish line, just to ensure i wouldn't delete it.

Bliss." 4

Dad jokes. When does a joke become a dad joke? When it's full groan.

Father and daughter climb Mt. Everest. Chhamji Sherpa, a 16-year-old is the youngest female to reach the summit of Everest taking the South Side route according to the Guinness Book of World Records. Her father, Dendi Sherpa, a professional Mt. Everest guide assisted his daughter, Chhamji. They are also the first father-daughter team to reach the top of Everest. [5]

Show don't tell. "Good fathers not only tell us how to live, but also they show us."

-- Mark Twain

Raising daughters. "To be the father of growing daughters is to understand something of what Yeats evokes with his imperishable phrase 'terrible beauty.' Nothing can make one so happily exhilarated or so frightened."

— Christopher Hitchens, Hitch 22: A Memoir

Things my dad would not say.

- "Go ahead and take my new sports car. I just washed it. Wait, here's 100 bucks for gas!"

- "Those tattoos look great! I'll get the same one and my ears pierced too!"

- "I enjoy Monday Night Football, but here's the TV remote. Watch whatever you want to."

- "I'm not going to drink beer anymore."

- "You relax, take your shoes off and watch TV. I'll jump out and mow the lawn! I might wash the car I gave you too."

Sex talk from dad. "My father tried to give me the sex talk once, and he apparently chickened out. He walked into my room and went, 'Adam -- uh, don't kiss guys.'"

– Adam Farrar, Comedian

Cycle. "A father is always making his baby into a little woman. And when she is a woman, he turns her back again."

— Enid Bagnold

Get a lock. Mom walked in on me and an ex-girlfriend getting it on and flipped out. She told my dad (they were divorced) hoping he'd talk some sense into me.

He said five words about it, "Next time get a lock."

-- Unknown

A great man died today. He wasn't a world leader or a famous doctor or a war hero or a sports figure. He was no business tycoon, and you will never see his name in the financial pages. But he was one of the greatest men who ever lived. He was my father. I guess you might say he was a person who was never interested in getting credit or receiving honors. He did corny things like pay bills on time, go to church on Sunday and serve as an officer in the P.T.A.

He helped his kids with their homework and drove his wife to do the grocery shopping on Thursday nights. He got a great kick out of hauling his teenagers and their friends to and from football games.

Tonight, is my first night without him. I don't know what to do with myself. I am sorry now for the times I didn't show him the proper respect. But I am grateful for a lot of other things.

I am thankful to have had my father for 15 years. And I am happy that I was able to let him know how much I loved him. That wonderful man died with a smile on his face and fulfillment in his heart. He knew that he was a great success as a husband and a father, a brother, a son, and a friend.

-- Anon.

The difference between a son and a daughter. "A son is a son till he gets a wife.

"A daughter is a daughter for the rest of her life."

– Irish saying.

Friend and role model. "My dad was my best friend and greatest role model. He was an amazing dad, coach, mentor, soldier, husband and friend."

– Tiger Woods

Don't tell me about numbers! Four expectant fathers were in a Minneapolis hospital waiting room, while their wives were in labor.

The nurse tells the first man, "Congratulations! You're the father of twins!"

"What a coincidence! I work for the Minnesota Twins baseball team!"

The nurse returns and tells the second man, "You are the father of triplets!"

"Wow, what a coincidence! I work for 3M Corporation!"

The nurse then tells the third man that his wife has given birth to quadruplets.

"Another coincidence! I work at the Four Seasons Hotel!"

At this point, the fourth guy faints. When he comes to, the others ask what's wrong.

"What's wrong?! I work for Seven-Up."

Say what? "My father calls me up, and says, 'If you need cash, make a collect call from 'Hugh Broke'. That way I'll wire you the money, but I won't have to pay for the long-distance phone call.'

"So, whatever, I followed his instructions. I made a collect call from 'Hugh Broke.'

A minute later, my phone rings: 'We have a person-to-person call for Mr. Hugh Broke from Mr. Rob Bank.'"

-- Hugh Fink, Comedian

Slip of the tongue. "Funny thing about my late Dad, I was told that while he and my mother were on their honeymoon, he went to the reception at the place where they were staying and asked if they had seen his girlfriend."

The receptionist said, 'No, but your wife has just gone back to your room.'

'Oh,' said Dad, 'I forgot I just got married.'"

-- Beverley Wrenn

Learn a trade. "My childhood was really nice. My parents never forced me to do anything; it was always, 'If you want to do that, fine.' So, when I told my father I was going to be an actor, he said, 'Fine, but study welding just in case.'"

-- Robin Williams

Pat of butter. "The father of a daughter is nothing but a high-class hostage.

"A father turns a stony face to his sons, berates them, shakes his antlers, paws the ground, snorts, runs them off into the underbrush…

"But when his daughter puts her arm over his shoulder and says, 'Daddy, I need to ask you something,' he is a pat of butter in a hot frying pan."

-- Garrison Keillor

Who started Father's Day? Sonora Louise Smart Dodd (1882 – 1978), the daughter of an American Civil War Veteran, who started it after listening to a sermon about the newly recognized Mother's Day in Church. She spearheaded at her church celebrating Father's Day in 1909 to honor fathers. She wanted it to be on June 5th of each year as that was her father's birthday. But the Alliance at her church decided on the third Sunday in June. Father's Day became popular and later embraced across the nation. [6]

Let's go drinking. "I don't have a kid, but I think that I would be a good father, especially if my baby liked to go out drinking."

– Eugene Mirman, Comedian

The cat's out of the bag. "When our cat, Taffy, died, Dad buried her under a tree in the back yard. A few nights later Mum went into the garden and found that the dog had dug Taffy up and eaten one of its legs.

"She woke Dad up, so he went out in PJs and army boots with a shovel over his shoulder and re-dug the hole. But because it was late, he decided to get rid of the towel he'd originally wrapped Taffy in and chucked it aside. He then reburied the cat and went back to bed.

"The next morning, Mum discovered that he'd chucked the cat aside and buried the towel."

– Yuki Sayeg

Do you want to discover your children's general knowledge? Try this game. Sit with your children and play music.

Give one of them something they can pass to each other such as a toy microphone, or a ball - whatever is handy, and tell them you are going to give them a topic and the one holding the microphone or other object must come up with a word or phrase about the topic.

For example, a few topics you can start with could be,

- Words that begin with "S"
- Names of different cars
- Names of different pets
- Names of different languages
- Names of different sports
- Different types of music, etc.

After you give the first child the object and a topic, see what answers that child comes up with. After the first child is through, he or she passes the object to the next child and the next child must likewise come up with a word or phrase about that subject, and the process continues until you stop the music.

When the music stops, the one holding the object must talk for 30 seconds more about that topic.

Then start again with another topic.

You may be surprised at how much they know!

Al Unser. "Dad taught me everything I know. Unfortunately, he didn't teach me everything he knows."

    -- Al Unser Jr.

Learning the order of numbers. The teacher asks little Johnny if he knows his numbers.

"Yes," he says. "My daddy taught me."

"Can you tell me what comes after three?"

"Four," answers little Johnny.

"What comes after six?"

"Seven," answers little Johnny.

"Very good," says the teacher. "Your father did a very fine job.

What comes after ten?"

"A jack," answers little Johnny.

Dad? "The average American may not know who his grandfather was. But the American was, however, one degree better off than the average Frenchman who, as a rule, was in considerable doubt as to who his father was."

-- Mark Twain

Don't clap. "There should be a children's song: 'If you're happy and you know it, keep it to yourself and let dad sleep.'"

-- Jim Gaffigan

Shooting beavers. This is an old one, but you might not have heard it. The Old Man and the Beaver. An 86-year-old man went to his doctor for his quarterly check-up... The doctor asked him how he was feeling, and the 86-year-old said, "Things are great and I've never felt better. I now have a 20-year-old bride who is pregnant with my child. So, what do you think about that Doc?"

The doctor considered his question for a minute and then began to tell a story. "I have an older friend, much like you, who is an avid hunter and never missed a hunting season. One day he was setting off to go hunting. In a bit of a hurry, he accidentally picked up his walking cane instead of his gun. As he neared a lake, he came across a very large male beaver sitting at the water's edge. He realized he'd left his gun at home and so he couldn't shoot the magnificent creature. Out of habit he raised his cane, aimed it at the animal as if it were his hunting rifle, and said, "bang, bang! Miraculously, two shots rang out and the beaver fell over dead. Now, what do you think of that?" asked the doctor.

The 86-year-old said, "Logic would strongly suggest that somebody else pumped a couple of rounds into that beaver."

The doctor replied, "My point exactly!"

Walks it instead of talks it. "A father doesn't tell you that he loves you. He shows you."

—Dimitri the Stoneheart

Great fathers. "The greatest mark of a father is how he treats his children when no one is looking."

—Dan Pearce

Father's Day gift from a daughter. "Dad, your Father's Day gift is another year of not having to pay for my wedding."

Doesn't matter. "It doesn't matter who my father was; it matters who I remember he was."

—Anne Sexton

Embarrassed dad! When I was in the 7th grade, I was solving my math homework with my mom in the early evening after dinner. It was still light outside and I wanted to go outside and play with my friends at least until about 8pm. Mom insisted I do my homework first. So, I was miserable.

Then mom left the room, and my dad came in and saw how unhappy I was, so he made a secret deal. He would finish my homework and I could go out and play with my friends.

When I got that homework back from the teacher, there was a note saying I failed, and she was very surprised as that was unusual for me. I told her my dad helped me with my homework and she asked me what my dad did for a living. I told her he was a lawyer and she laughed and laughed, and so did mom when she found out.

Dad said he did it fast and assumed the teacher would easily see that the reasoning was correct.

I told him -- she only looks at the bottom-line answer when she corrects homework.

Dad has been banned from doing homework.

-- Anon.

Fishing and shopping. "It is admirable for a man to take his son fishing, but there is a special place in heaven for the father who takes his daughter shopping."

— John Sinor

A child's laugh. "We wondered why when a baby laughed, he belonged to Daddy, and when he had a sagging diaper that smelled like a landfill, 'He wants his mother.'"

-- Erma Bombeck

A few dad jokes.

A termite walks into a bar and asks, "Is the bar tender here?"

My friend keeps saying, "Cheer up man it could be worse, you could be stuck underground in a hole full of water." I know he means well.

What is Beethoven's favorite fruit? A ba-na-na-naaaa.

Did you hear the rumor about butter? I really shouldn't be spreading it.

My wife said I should do lunges to stay in shape. That would be a big step forward.

"My daughter screeched, 'Daaaaaad, you haven't listened to one word I've said, have you!?' What a strange way to start a conversation with me."

I told my son I'm named after Thomas Jefferson. He says, but dad, your name is Brian. I respond, I know, but I was named AFTER Thomas Jefferson.

Why do chicken coops only have two doors? Because if they had four, they would be chicken sedans.

Why did the Clydesdale give the pony a glass of water? Because he was a little horse.

A dad died due to us not being able to remember his blood type. As he died, he kept insisting that we "be positive" but it's hard without him.

Don't trust atoms. They make up everything!

I've got a great pizza joke for you. Never mind, it's too cheesy.

Did you hear about the guy who invented Lifesavers? They say he made a mint.

I stayed up all night wondering where the sun had gone. And then it dawned on me.

Taller. "Dad, I may be taller than you now…but I still look up to you."

-- Anon.

Father-daughter one-handed crack an egg world record.

Gordon Ramsay and his daughter, Matilda entered a contest to see what father-daughter team could, using only one hand, crack the most eggs in one minute. They fell slightly short of breaking the 28-egg one-handed egg cracks in one minute.

The current Guinness World Record is held by Washington restauranteur, Ross McCurdy, and his daughter for the 28 eggs cracked one-handed in a minute record by a team of two. [7]

If you have a day with nothing to do, teach your kids how to break an egg using one hand.

No equal. "No man I ever met was my father's equal, and I never loved any other man as much."

— Hedy Lamarr, Hollywood Walk of Fame Actress

Stand by me. "She did not stand alone, but what stood behind her, the most potent moral force in her life, was the love of her father."

—Harper Lee

Bored with the kids at home? (CAUTION: These may be highly dangerous to try and use them at your own risk with all proper safeguards).

Get in the record books by trying to break a world record.

Here is a list of world records that might interest you and your children. These are from the Guinness World Record book. (Please always check online for the current record at the time you decide at your own risk to attempt any of these as these records change).

These records range from the almost impossible to perhaps something you and your kids could try after training and practicing. Training and practicing help kids learn self-discipline. Discuss and set up a training schedule with your kids.

The first one is tough except for the most adept at the cube.

The Fastest Time to Solve 3 Rubik's Cubes Simultaneously Using Hands and Feet. Que Jianyun from Xiamen, Fujian Province, China holds the record for 1 minute 36.39 seconds!

Most Ice Cream Scoops Balanced on One Cone. Italian Dimitri Panciera set a record for 125 scoops on a cone balanced for 10 seconds.

Most Four-leafed Clovers Picked in One Minute. Record held by American Katie Borka who in 2018 picked 166 in 60 minutes (1 hour) in Virginia.

This one is interesting! Most T-Shirts Worn at Once. Record held by Canadian Ted Hastings – who wore 260 t-shirts on 17 Feb 2019 (Makes you wonder how many people actually have 261 t-shirts?).

Keeping Two Balloons in the Air Using Only Your Head. Abhinabha Tangerman from the Netherlands kept two balloons using only his head in the air for 1 minute 9 seconds in 2018.

Tallest Lego Brick Criss-Cross Tower Built in 30 seconds with One Hand. The record holder is Italian Silvia Sabba who built a 29-block Lego-brick tower in 30 seconds.

Most Plastic Bottle Caps Stacked into a Tower in One Minute. Italian Silvia Sabba stacked 43 in one minute.

Most CDs Balanced on One Finger. Italian Silvia Sabba from Italy balanced 247 in total.

Most Spoons Balanced on the Face at One Time. Serbian Dalibor Jablanovic held 31 spoons on his face for 5 seconds.

Most Toilet Rolls Balanced on the Head. Twelve toilet rolls balanced for 30 seconds.

Most Blindfolded Plastic Bottle Flips in One Minute. American Josh Horton did 27 full flips in one minute while blindfolded and the bottle landed perfectly on each flip.

Most Baked Beans Eaten in One Minute -- Using Chopsticks. Japanese Cherry Yoshitake ate 71 in 2015. [8]

Who's the boss? While having their evening dinner together, a little girl looked up at her father and asked, "Daddy, you're the boss in our family, right?"

The father was very pleased to hear it and confidently replied, "Yes, my little princess."

The girl then continued, "That's because mommy put you in charge, right?"

– Unknown

Father's Day tradition. By tradition, fathers wear a red flower on Father's Day, if their father is alive and a white flower if he's dead.

And if they have a nagging wife and a house full of screaming kids, they wear a pink flower - which means they are living but are half--dead.

– Unknown

Don't need drugs. "You don't need drugs when you have a baby in the home. You're awake, you're paranoid, you smell bad… it's the same thing."

–Robin Williams

Dad is into Peppa pig. "It's a very LSD-trip phase of my life. My daughter is obsessed with Peppa Pig. This is my life. There are three women who do the voice the character of Peppa Pig.

"And she's a pig.

"Hello?

"And I'm so deep down into that crevasse right now that I have opinions on which actress is the best Peppa."

– Alec Baldwin

Frat house. "Having children is like living in a frat house. Nobody sleeps, everything's broken and there's a lot of throwing up."

– Ray Romano

Slip of the tongue.

Son: "For $20, I'll be good."

Dad: "Oh, yeah? When I was your age, I was good for nothing."

It's not too late! How old was the oldest father? According to the Guinness Book of World Records, the oldest man ever to father a child was reportedly Aussie Les Colley (1898 - 1998), who had his ninth child -- a son named Oswald -- with his third wife at the age of 92 years 10 months. Les met Oswald's Fijian mother in 1991 through a dating agency at the age of 90. [9]

However, according to Wikipedia, Ramjit Raghav (1916 – 2020) was a British Raj-Indian wrestler, farmer and vegetarian who unofficially claimed to be the world's oldest father. He resided in southern India with his wife and claimed to have had his first child with his wife at age 94. [10]

Ramjit also claimed to be the father of a second child at age 96. He was a vegetarian who claimed to engage in sexual intercourse around three times a day. [11]

Disappointing looks. "In the 'looks of disappointment' department, my cat has picked up where my father left off."

　-- Tom Papa

Dad is real. "It's a wonderful feeling when your father becomes not a god but a man to you - when he comes down from the mountain and you see he's this man with weaknesses. And you love him as his whole being, not as a figurehead."

　-- Robin Williams

Support. "When my father didn't have my hand, he had my back."

– Linda Poindexter

God took the strength of a mountain and

The majesty of a tree,

The warmth of a summer sun,

The calm of a quiet sea,

The generous soul of nature,

The comforting arm of night,

The wisdom of the ages,

The power of the eagle's flight,

The joy of a morning in spring,

The faith of a mustard seed,

The patience of eternity,

For the Father Who Has Everything by Team Golfwell

The depth of a family need,

Then God combined these qualities,

And there was nothing more to add,

He knew His masterpiece was complete,

And so, he called it – Dad.

-- Brie Carter

New baby on the way? Prepare to slow down on the sex and bungee jumping. After your wife becomes pregnant, a dad's testosterone decreases according to a study done by the National Academy of Sciences of the United States. [12]

More bad news. After the child is born fathers are less likely to engage in high-risk activities. Probably tough to take the baby cliff climbing, parasailing, etc. [13]

Dad's advice. "He's got all kinds of advice about show biz. He says, 'It's just like sales. You gotta make your opportunities. You gotta take your opportunities. You remember what Jesus said? You give a man a fish, that man knows where to come for fish. You teach a man to fish, and you just destroyed your market base.'"

-- Jackie Kashian, Comedian

What's hard about being a dad? "I would say the hardest thing about being a parent is these goddamn kids."

-- Andy Richter, Comedian

What happens at 12 weeks after being born? "12 weeks old: when your kid is young enough to fall asleep on your chest yet long enough to kick you in the nuts at the same time."

-- Lin-Manuel Miranda

They may not say it but "Every son quotes his father, in words, or if not in words, then in deeds."

— Terri Guillemets

Some dad jokes you may not have heard before.

There are three guys on a boat, and they have four cigarettes, but nothing to light them with – what do they do?
They throw one cigarette overboard, and the boat becomes a cigarette lighter.

Accordian to a recent survey, replacing words with the names of musical instruments often goes undetected…

For the Father Who Has Everything by Team Golfwell

What has four letters, sometimes has nine letters, and never has five letters…

A slice of apple pie is $2.50 in Jamaica and $3 in the Bahamas…
There are the pie rates of the Caribbean.

The other day I bought a thesaurus, but when I got home and opened it, all the pages were blank…
I have no words to describe how angry I am.

I hope Elon Musk never gets involved in a scandal…
Elon-gate would be really drawn out.

I met some chess players in the hotel lobby. They were bragging about how good they were…
It was chess nuts boasting in an open foyer.

I started a band called 999 megabytes…
We still haven't gotten a gig.

To the person who stole my copy of Microsoft Office, I will find you…
You have my Word…

A man is washing the car with his son. The son asks…
"Dad, can't you just use a sponge?"

I invited my girlfriend to the gym with me and then didn't show up…
I hope she gets the message that we're not working out.

"Hey dad, have you seen my sunglasses?"
"No, have you seen my dad glasses?"

The police just pulled me over, and the officer came up to my window and said "papers?"
I said "scissors, I win!" and drove off. He's been chasing me for 45 minutes now, I think he wants a rematch.

Indescribable. "Fatherhood is the greatest thing that could ever happen. You can't explain it until it happens; it's like telling somebody what water feels like before they've ever swam in it."

—Michael Bublé

85-year-old dad sets Mount Kilimanjaro climb record

Robert Wheeler climbed Mount Kilimanjaro at the age of 85 with his son. They accomplished the climb over several days, and they plan to do it again on Dad's 90th birthday. [14]

That is an amazing feat as many men of this age might have difficulty making it to the bathroom in the middle of the night.

Before Robert attempted the record-making climb, he trained with his son Jack. After days of climbing, both father and son made it to the very top, accomplishing a feat no other dad had ever done at Robert's age. [15]

For the Father Who Has Everything by Team Golfwell

Mount Kilimanjaro, Tanzania 19,341 ft.

War? "Yes, I've been to war, and I've raised twins. If I had a choice, I'd rather go to war."

-- George W. Bush (who raised twin daughters)

Different father? A dying husband in a hospital bed asks his wife, "Our seventh child always looked different from the other six. Did he have a different father?"

His wife, crying uncontrollably answers, "Yes."

He asks, "Whose is it?"

His wife replies, "Yours!"

"I do like a proper hug and snuggle but it's tough getting it from the kids. You can get it when they first wake up and they're disoriented; then it's a possibility. But other than that, they're always moving, they're dipping, they're slipping, they're embarrassed, and running away."

–Mark Wahlberg

A father called his five small children together... The children gathered and sat together in a circle on the floor. Then dad placed a toy in the middle.

He explained to them that he won this toy as a door prize, and he wanted to give it to one of them.

He asked them "Who is the most obedient?"

Five sets of eyes looked up at him. Sensing that they didn't understand the word, "obedient", he asked, "Ok, who always obeys mommy, and does everything she says?"

One of the children picked up the toy and handed it to dad. "You win!" exclaimed the child.

Want an ambitious daughter? Psychologists at the University of British Columbia studied the success of daughters whose fathers performed household chores (dishes, laundry, etc.)

and found that those daughters are more likely to follow business or professional careers like being a CEO or lawyer. [16]

Where does the moon go? "On our 6 a.m. walk, my daughter asked where the moon goes each morning. I let her know it's in heaven visiting daddy's freedom."

--Ryan Reynolds

Dads are ordinary men turned by love into heroes, adventurers, storytellers, and singers of songs.

-- Anon.

Treat them like sons. "You don't raise heroes, you raise sons. And if you treat them like sons, they'll turn out to be heroes, even if it's just in our own eyes."

— Walter M. Schirra, Sr.

How much? "If you had a dollar," quizzed the teacher, "and you asked your father for another dollar and fifty cents, how much money would you have?"

"One dollar." answered little Johnny.

"You don't know your basic math." said the teacher shaking her head, disappointed.

Little Johnny shook his head too, "You don't know my daddy."

Roses are tough,

        Violets don't quit,

        When it comes to being a dad,

        You should really know your sh…

Move over. "One time, my own father caught me watching a porno movie. The one thing you don't want to hear in that situation is, 'Son, move over.'"

– Dave Attell, Comedian

Hint, Hint.

Dear Dad,

$chool i$ really great. I am making lot$ of friend$ and $tudying very hard. With all my $tuff, I $imply can't think of anything I need, $o if you would like, you can ju$t $end me a card, a$ I would love to hear from you.

Love,

Your $on

Dear Son, I kNOw that astroNOmy, ecoNOmics, and oceaNOgraphy are eNOugh to keep even an hoNOr student busy. Do NOt forget that the pursuit of kNOwledge is a NOble task, and you can never study eNOugh.

Love,

Dad

Thank you from your daughter. "Thank you, Dad. You are always someone who knew long before I did what boys I dated were jerks."

    – Anon.

How true. "By the time a man realizes that maybe his father was right, he usually has a son who thinks he's wrong."

— Charles Wadsworth

Happy (technical) Father's Day! I got you a present but if you want to get technical then technically you bought it.

By the way, can I borrow $20?

– Anon.

Want lots of kids? Legend says, Genghis Khan fathered over a thousand children from a large harem of women he whom he captured or acquired in some other way, reaching numbers of about 2,000 to 3,000 women. Scientists in the Russian Academy of Sciences estimate he has 16 million male descendants living today in Central Asia. That would be a very confusing Father's Day for Genghis getting cards from places he'd hadn't ever been to?!

According to the Guinness Book of World Records, for polygamous countries, the number of descendants can become incalculable. For example, at the time of his death on 15 October 1992, Samuel S. Mast, aged 96, of Fryburg, Pennsylvania, had 824 living descendants from 11 children, 97 grandchildren, 634 great-grandchildren and 82 great-great-grandchildren. [17]

The last Sharifian Emperor of Morocco, Moulay Ismail (1672–1727), known as "The Bloodthirsty", was reputed to have fathered a total of 525 sons and 342 daughters by 1703 and achieved a 700th son in 1721. [18]

Drive thru. "We see a McDonald's. We got so excited. We started chanting, 'McDonald's, McDonald's, McDonald's!'

And my dad pulled into the drive-thru and we started cheering!

And then, he ordered one black coffee for himself… and kept driving.

My dad is cold-blooded."

    -- John Mulaney, Comedian

Good father. "A good father is one of the most unsung, unpraised, unnoticed, and yet one of the most valuable assets in our society."

    — Billy Graham

Storyteller. God created the mule, and told him, "You will be mule, working constantly from dusk to dawn, carrying heavy loads on your back. You will eat grass and lack intelligence. You will live for 50 years."

The mule answered, "To live like this for 50 years is too much. Please, give me no more than 20." And it was so.

Then God created the dog, and told him, "You will hold vigilance over the dwellings of Man, to whom you will be his greatest companion. You will eat his table scraps and live for 25 years."

And the dog responded, "Lord, to live 25 years as a dog like that is too much. Please, no more than 10 years." And it was so.

God then created the monkey, and told him, "You are monkey. You shall swing from tree to tree, acting like an idiot. You will be funny, and you shall live for 20 years."

And the monkey responded, "Lord, to live 20 years as the clown of the world is too much. Please, Lord, give me no more than 10 years." And it was so.

Finally, God created Man and told him, "You are Man, the only rational being that walks the earth. You will use your intelligence to have mastery over the creatures of the world. You will dominate the earth and live for 20 years."

And the man responded, "Lord, to be Man for only 20 years is too little. Please, Lord, give me the 30 years the mule refused, the 15 years the dog refused, and the 10 years the monkey rejected." And it was so.

And so, God made Man to live 20 years as a man, then marry and become a husband and live 30 years like a mule working and carrying heavy loads on his back. Then, he is to become a dad and have children and live 15 years as a dog, guarding his house and eating the leftovers after they empty the pantry; then, in his old age, to live 10 years as a monkey, acting like an idiot to amuse his grandchildren.

And God was pleased with his creations.

What we become. "I believe that what we become depends on what our fathers try to teach us at odd moments, when they aren't trying to teach us. We are formed by little scraps of wisdom."

-- Umberto Eco, Italian philosopher

The real thrill. "The thrill of being a great father is not seeing your children go on to become successful adults. The thrill of a great father is the journey, experiencing your child's successes along the pathway to their greatness."

—Reed Markham

Marathon running. Are you and your sons or daughters into marathon running? The record time for a marathon run by a parent and a child is held by Irishmen Tommy Hughes and Eoin Hughes who ran this record time at the 2019 Frankfurt, Germany Marathon, on 27 October 2019. Their aggregate time was 4 hr 59 min 22 sec. Dad is a regular long-distance runner who represented Ireland in the 1992 Summer Olympics. Eoin is his son. [19]

It's bedtime.

Dad: "Mom told you to stay in bed."

Three-Year-old: "There's a scary monster in my closet."

Dad: Scarier than mom?"

Three-year-old goes to bed.

Living up to dad. "I've always felt sorry for Jesus 'cause you know no matter what he ever did, he could never live up to his father."

-- Gilbert Gottfried, Comedian

Sissy Magazine? When he was a teenager, Johnny's father caught him reading one of his older sister's magazines. "Why are you reading that sissy magazine?" he asked.

"There's an article that tells women where to meet men," Johnny said pointing to the magazine's cover. "And I need to know where I'm supposed to be."

-- Unknown

Teaching sons. "When you teach your son, you teach your son's son."

— The Talmud

Rainy day stuff to do with small kids. Here are a few fun things. This list can be infinitely long, and these will usually lead to more activities for Dads to do with small children.

- Read them a silly story like The Wonky Donkey, etc.

- Piggyback rides.

- Pretend they are a pillow and put your head on their belly.

- Show them how to dance.

- Pretend to be the sleeping, silent monster not to be awakened and let them bravely creep up on you.

- Sing silly songs. Yakety Yak, Purple People Eater, Monster Mash, etc.

- Take silly pictures or videos of each other.

- Look them in the eyes and tell them how much you love them.

Can't help but do this. "Listen, there is no way any true man is going to let children live around him in his home and not discipline them and teach them how to fight, and mold them until they know all he knows. His goal is to make them better than he is. Being their friend is a distant second to this."

— Victor Devlin

Daddy issues? Not my daughter. "My daughter doesn't have any daddy issues, but I can guarantee her boyfriend will."

– Unknown

Who? A young boy is listening to the radio in the car with his father. "Dad, what music did you like growing up?"

"I was a huge fan of The Rolling Stones."

"The who?" the son asks.

"Yeah," the dad responds, "I liked them too."

For the Father Who Has Everything by Team Golfwell

What is a dad?

A dad is someone who
wants to catch you before you fall
but instead picks you up,
brushes you off,
and lets you try again.

A dad is someone who
wants to keep you from making mistakes
but instead lets you find your own way,
even though his heart breaks in silence
when you get hurt.

A dad is someone who
holds you when you cry,
scolds you when you break the rules,
shines with pride when you succeed,
and has faith in you even when you fail…

-- Anon.

Stories about dads. **Hide the presents.** "My dad always went out of his way to make our birthday parties special. One year, he hid the presents from my sister and me, prank-called us and told us they had been stolen, then sent us on a scavenger hunt with our party guests to find them!"

-- Grace Elkus

"It's grandma. When I was eight years old, I was called into the principal's office and my father was looking very solemn. And he said, 'We gotta go, it's Grandma.'

"We got in the car, and I said, 'What's wrong with Grandma?' And he said, 'Nothing, we're going to the movies.'"

-- Sam Rockwell, Actor

Our song. "When I was little my dad would sometimes sing the song 'Sweet Baby James,' by James Taylor, to me as a lullaby before falling asleep. And once or twice he even played guitar along with it. I loved it so much that I chose it for our father-daughter dance at my wedding 12 years ago, and now I sing it to my boys as a lullaby. It will always be our song."

-- Naomi Lindberg

Dad's surprise. "When I was 10 years old, I was in a swimming race from school. My mom couldn't come to watch, with three young children at home and my dad was at work. Although I was a very good swimmer, I didn't really care about the race since my parents would not be there. But halfway through the race I heard my dad's voice yelling out, "Go girl, I am here."

He had slipped away from work to be there. So, I sprinted as hard as I could, as I was behind in the race and didn't want to disappoint my dad.

I had two laps to go and finished up winning my race – and the next one.

I adored my dad. He taught me to swim when I was two years of age. He helped me always and encouraged me to dive off a 10-meter board. Great memories still last all this time, and I am now 86 years old.

-- Liberta Mitten

Benefits. "Fathering is not something perfect men do, but something that perfects the man."

— Frank Pittman

Riding on your shoulders. "You used to pick me up and let me ride on your shoulders and now I'm proud to stand on them as everything I am I owe to your guidance, protection, and love."

-- Anon.

On dad's shoulders

Dad: "Son, if you keep pulling my hair, you will have to get off my shoulders."

Son: "But, Dad, I'm just trying to get my gum back!"

Best years. "You can tell what the best years of your father's life were, because they seem to freeze that clothing style and ride it out."

-- Jerry Seinfeld

Smart dad! "Happy Father's Day to a dad who was smart enough to teach me how to mow the lawn so he wouldn't have to."

-- Unknown

Love. "I rescind my early statement, 'I could never fall in love with a girl who regularly poops her pants.' Why, do I say this? Well, I hadn't met my daughter yet."

-- Dax Shephard, Actor, Comedian, and writer.

Single dads. "Saturday mornings, I've learned, are a great opportunity for kids to sneak into your bed, fall back asleep, and kick you in the face."

— Dan Pearce, from "Single Dad Laughing"

Titles. "Of all the titles I've been privileged to have, 'Dad' has always been the best."

— Ken Norton, Former WBC Heavyweight Boxing Champion.

Got to know dad. My father retired to San Francisco, and I got a chance to know him and be around him. It's always been someplace where everything changed for the better. It's always been a home for me.

– Robin Williams

Connection. "With sons and fathers, there's an inexplicable connection and imprint that your father leaves on you."

— Brad Pitt

How fathers were created. "When the good Lord was creating Fathers, he started with a tall frame.

"A female angel nearby said, 'What kind of a father is that? If you're going to make children so close to the ground, why have you put the father up so high? He won't be able to shoot marbles without kneeling, tuck a child in bed without bending, or even kiss a child without stooping.'

God smiled and said, 'Yes, but if I make him child size, who would children have to look up to?'

And when God made a father's hands, they were large. The angel shook her head and said, 'Large hands can't manage diaper pins, small buttons, rubber bands on ponytails, or even remove splinters caused from baseball bats.'

Again, God smiled and said, 'I know, but they're large enough to hold everything a small boy empties from his pockets, yet small enough to cup a child's face in them.'

Then God molded long slim legs and broad shoulders, 'Do you realize you just made a father without a lap?' The angel chuckled.

God said, 'A mother needs a lap. A father needs strong shoulders to pull a sled, to balance a boy on a bicycle, or to hold a sleepy head on the way home from the circus.'

When God was in the middle of creating the biggest feet anyone had ever seen, the angel could not contain herself any longer. 'That's not fair. Do you honestly think those feet are going to get out of bed early in the morning when the baby cries, or walk through a birthday party without crushing one or two of the guests?'

God again smiled and said, 'They will work. You will see. They will support a small child who wants to ride to Banbury Cross or scare mice away from a summer cabin, or display shoes that will be a challenge to fill.'

God worked throughout the night, giving the father few words, but a firm authoritative voice and eyes that see everything, but remain calm and tolerant.

Finally, almost as an afterthought, He added tears. Then he turned to the angel and said, 'Now are you satisfied he can love as much as a mother can?'

The angel said nothing more."

-- Erma Bombeck

Drinking fountain fact. Halsey Taylor invented the drinking fountain in 1912. He did this for his father, who died of typhoid fever after drinking from a contaminated public water supply in 1896. [20]

Daughters growing up. "To be the father of growing daughters is to understand something of what Yeats evokes with his imperishable phrase 'terrible beauty.' Nothing can make one so happily exhilarated or so frightened: It's a solid lesson in the limitations of self to realize that your heart is running around inside someone else's body."

-- Christopher Hitchens

How many fathers and sons have been US Presidents? Only 2 sets of father-son US Presidents so far. John Adams (2nd) and son John Quincy Adams (6th). George Bush (41st) and son George W. Bush (43rd).

Double standard. **Son**: "Dad I got a girlfriend."
Dad: "Go Johnny go!"

Daughter: "Dad I got a boyfriend."
Dad loads shotgun.

Beyond words. "My father's heart is too full, and no words to release it."

— Gabrielle Zevin

Can a dad be pregnant? One definition of the word "pregnant" means "to carry a baby or babies."

Male seahorses (and their close relatives, the male pipefish, and male seadragons) get pregnant and give birth to babies. The dads carry the eggs and fertilize the eggs.

The way it works is that the male seahorse has a front pouch. Males and females dance around one another, fluttering their fins over several days, then mate. When mating, the female seahorse deposits up to 1,500 eggs in the male's pouch.

The dad carries the eggs until the babies are born usually within 45 days and tiny baby seahorses emerge fully developed. [21]

Tough taking the temperature. "I was told that I needed to check her temperature through the rectum. I was like, 'No. Can't be.' There's a mouth, there's an armpit, there's got to be something else...

"The doctor was like, 'No, no, no, just have one of you guys distract her, and the other one does it. She'll be fine'...

It all went well though. I didn't lose it. It came back out."

-- Ryan Reynolds

Why is dad the enemy? "Every commercial goes after the father. It's like, 'America Online is so easy, even Dad can use it.' You mean the guy who bought you the f**king computer?"

-- Nick DiPaola, Comedian

Need money? "I know when my kids need money because that's when they laugh at my jokes."

– Anon.

Pretending?

Mom: "She's wearing her princess dress. Pretend you're her servant."

Dad: "Honey, I don't have to pretend."

A picture is worth a thousand words. "A father carries pictures where his money used to be."

– Steve Martin

Putting kids to bed is easy. I don't get why people think getting kids to bed is hard – all my son needs are,

- A drink of water
- 4 songs from Daddy
- A trip to the potty
- Superman flight to bed
- An inventory of his stuffed animals
- A tissue
- 2 more songs
- Look at my watch for 45 seconds
- And all these 7 more times

Unseen tears. "A father's tears and fears are unseen, his love is unexpressed, but his care and protection remain as a pillar of strength throughout our lives."

— Ama H. Vanniarachchy, Writer, Journalist

Losing weight. A Texan buys a round of drinks for the entire bar, announcing that his wife has just given birth to their first child "a typical Texas" baby boy weighing 24 pounds! Congratulations showered him from all around, along with many exclamations of "Wow!"

Two weeks later, the Texan returns to the bar. The bartender says, "Say, you're the father of the typical Texas baby that weighed 24 pounds at birth. How much does he weigh now?" The proud father answers, "18 pounds."

The bartender, puzzled and concerned, asks, "Why? What happened? He already weighed 24 pounds at birth."

The Texas father takes a slow swig from his longneck beer, wipes his lips on his shirt sleeve, leans into the bartender and proudly says, "Had him circumcised."

Or in other words. "It is easier for a father to have children than for children to have a real father."

-- Pope John XXIII

Diaper race! A study found mothers, on average, take 2 minutes 5 seconds to change a diaper, which is equivalent to about three 40-hour work weeks each year.

However, fathers are a bit more focused (or whatever) and take an average of 1 minute 36 seconds. [22]

Creation. "Being a dad is about creating a human when you aren't necessarily capable of putting together a bookcase without help."

– Anon.

Thank you, dad, from your daughter. "Daddy, thanks for being my hero, chauffeur, financial support, listener, life mentor, friend, guardian, and simply being there every time, I needed a hug."

— Agatha Stephanie Lin

Dancing dads. "I'm probably the most uncool guy that my daughters know -- as far as they are concerned anyway -- 'cause I'm Dad. I mean dads just aren't cool—especially when I dance! They don't want me to dance."

-- Tim McGraw

Great father. "Being a great father is like shaving. No matter how good you shaved today, you must do it again tomorrow."

-- Unknown

Plane rides. "I would rather drink a piping hot bowl of liquid rabies than get on a plane with my two children. At 2 years old they just have to rip all their clothes off and introduce themselves to everyone on the plane, it's just like, 'Please can we land in a farmer's field?'"

-- Ryan Reynolds

Fathers understand this. "You fathers will understand. You have a little girl. She looks up to you. You're her oracle. You're her hero. And then the day comes when she gets her first permanent wave and goes to her first real party, and from that day on, you're in a constant state of panic."

— Stanley T. Banks

Knowledge acquired too late. "Much of life, fatherhood included, is the story of knowledge acquired too late. If only I'd known then what I know now, how much smarter, abler, stronger, I would have been.

"But nothing really prepares you for kids, for the swells of emotion that roll through your chest like the rumble of boulders tumbling downhill, nor for the all-enveloping labor of it, the sheer mulish endurance you need for the six or seven hundred discrete tasks that have to be done each day. Such a small person! Not much bigger than a loaf of bread at first, yet it takes so much to keep the whole enterprise going.

"Logistics, skills, materiel; the only way we really learn is by figuring it out as we go along, and even then, it changes on us every day, so we're always improvising, which is a fancy way of saying that we're doing things we technically don't know how to do."

— Ben Fountain

Example. "My father didn't tell me how to live. He lived and let me watch him do it."

— Clarence Budington Kelland

How do you figure? "My two-year-old can figure out how to work the TV remote but can't find his mouth when eating spaghetti."

– Unknown.

"Everybody thinks their dad's jokes are corny. I don't get a free pass on that. In fact, my daughter said to me once, 'Most of your stuff isn't funny at all. But I'm always surprised you make it work.'

"I thought that was a pretty sophisticated way of attacking me."

– Judd Apatow, Comedian

First-time dad. "My wife told me today that I'm gonna become a father for the very first time. The bad news is we already have two kids."

– Brian Kiley, Comedian

This is all you have to do. "For fatherhood advice, try to look your child in the eye and get to know their name; that becomes important when you want something. And remember to feed them. That's about all you need."

– Will Ferrell

The poorest dad. "Sometimes the poorest man leaves his children the richest inheritance."

— Ruth E. Renkel

The richest dad. "A very rich person should leave his kids enough to do anything, but not enough to do nothing."

-- Warren Buffett

Most kids. Who had the most kids with one wife? Feodor Vasilyeva and Valentina Vasilyeva had 69 children – sixteen pairs of twins, seven sets of triplets and four sets of quadruplets – between 1725 and 1765, a total of 27 births. 67 of the 69 children were said to have survived infancy. The claim is somewhat disputed as records at this time were not very well kept. Valentina died at the age of 76 and Feodor had another 18 children with his second wife, who had 6 pairs of twins and 2 sets of triplets, making him a father of 87 children in total. There is more data about Feodor's children in the Guinness Book of World Records. [23]

Role model. "Being a role model is the most powerful form of educating ... too often fathers neglect it because they get so caught up in making a living, they forget to make a life."

-- John Wooden

Am I teaching her about the future? "I might not be preparing my lovely daughter enough for the future when she grows up. She might be forced to go out into the ruins and be a slave to *Thundra, The Spear Mistress* and she'll resent me the whole time. She'll be like, 'Oh, thanks a lot, Dad. What amazing life safety skills you taught me: Scooter riding and Blade Runner trivia? Thanks a lot.'"

-- Patton Oswalt, Comedian

A bit confused? A guy goes to the supermarket and notices an attractive woman waving at him.

She says hello.

He's rather taken aback because he can't place where he knows her from. So, he says, "Do you know me?"

To which she replies, "I think you're the father of one of my kids."

Now his mind travels back to the only time he has ever been unfaithful to his wife and says, "My God, are you the stripper from my bachelor party that I made love to on the pool table with all my buddies watching while your partner whipped my butt with wet celery?"

She looks into his eyes and says calmly, "No, I'm your son's teacher."

Delayed appreciation for dad. "It's only when you grow up and step back from him — or leave him for your own home — it's only then that you can measure his greatness and fully appreciate it."

— Margaret Truman

The one and only Rodney Dangerfield…

- "I remember the time I was kidnapped, and they sent a piece of my finger to my father. He said he wanted more proof."

- "My father carries around the picture of the kid who came with his wallet."

- "I come from a stupid family. My father worked in a bank. They caught him stealing pens."

Rodney Dangerfield (1921-2004)

Melts away. "When I come home, my daughter will run to the door and give me a big hug, and everything that's happened that day just melts away."

— Hugh Jackman

Security cameras catch dad's ghost. Norma Villa in the UK had been caring for her 75-year-old mother Teresa, who had been diagnosed with terminal cancer, for two months. They had been discussing transferring Teresa to hospice. Norma went to her room for a moment to relieve stress and lied down. As she was lying down, and to relieve stress, Norma started telling her thoughts out loud to her father who had died 10 years earlier.

The strange thing about it was at that moment, Norma got a notification on her phone, alerting her that movement had been detected on the front porch by her security camera. She checked the footage and saw, as she put it, "a ghostly figure' swoop down and sit on her swinging porch seat – in the exact spot where her dad had sat whenever he enjoyed a cigarette."

Norma said, "I felt at peace when I saw the video. The first thing that came to my mind was my dad - I instantly knew it was him. It brings me comfort to think it was my dad watching over us both. I think he was there to reassure me."

Norma added, "The security camera gives off a notification when there's something around. I expected it to be a cat or something of an animal type, but it was actually that. I kept rewinding it and I was like 'what is that?' I showed my mother and the first thing she said was 'they're coming for me'. She wasn't scared, she wasn't hallucinating at the time."

"I just said 'please don't talk like that'. She just smiled." Norma's mother passed a short time later and she finds comfort in the video that Mother is now with dad. [24]

"If you're my father and if you love me…"

From the movie "McClintock"

Becky McLintock (Stephanie Powers): "If you're my father, if you do love me, you'll shoot him… (referring to a new young man she just met named Devlin)"

McClintock (John Wayne): "Well, I'm your father and I sure love you, so... (he grabs a pistol from his cabinet and shoots Devlin)."

Becky McLintock: "You shot him! You really shot him! If…if… he…"

McLintock: (Interrupts) "If he dies, he will be the first man killed with a blank cartridge. We use this to start the races on the fourth."

-- John Wayne, McClintock 1963 movie

Just kidding! "When your wife is pregnant and you're expecting, everyone is like, 'It's incredible. Get ready, it's magic. It's the most life-changing experience you'll ever have. Brace yourself for heaven.' And then the second the baby comes and everyone is like, 'WELCOME TO HELL.'"

-- Andy Samberg

Show him the world. "A boy needs a father to show him how to be in the world. He needs to be given swagger, taught how to read a map so that he can recognize the roads that lead to life and the paths that lead to death, how to know what love requires, and where to find steel in the heart when life makes demands on us that are greater than we think we can endure."

— Ian Morgan Cron

What a father does. That's what a father does – he eases the burdens of those he loves. Saves the ones he loves from painful last images that might endure for a lifetime."

—George Saunders

How to be cool. Some psychologists suggest various ways of smoothing feelings by teaching a child to be mellow, i.e., how to develop good Emotional Intelligence (EQ).

These might be helpful to get a child to express what's going on.

- "It seems you're feeling sad about this. Is that the case?"

- "You look frustrated. Is that how you feel?"

- "I can see that you're angry right now. Is there anything else you're feeling?"

- "It seems to me you're unhappy, but I want to hear from you how you feel."

- "Tell me how you're feeling, and what's going on with you right now."

"Children learn about showing emotions by watching and listening to their parents. Emotion coaching is a way for you to deliberately teach your child healthy emotional expression. This strategy helps kids feel understood and increases connections between parents and children. Emotion coaching teaches kids that feelings are acceptable, and it enables them to learn how to control their expression of emotions." [25]

Dad could do that. "When I was little, I bragged about my firefighting father. I would say, my father will go to heaven, because if he went to hell, he would put out all the fires"

— Jodi Picoult, from "My Sister's Keeper"

I'm thinking… "Do I miss having time to myself and sleeping through the night since my kid was born? Yes. But would I give up being a father just for the sake of the extra time in bed on the weekends, is that what you're asking me?

...Hang on I'm thinking..."

– Unknown

Great moments. "I mean, everything can be a great moment as a dad, especially when I'm gone as much as I am. I work a lot so, man, those weekends at home with my son are the greatest. I took him on a zombie cruise last year which was fun. And all he wanted to do was get zombie makeup put on. And so, he looked in the mirror at the reflection and he fainted!

"We probably won't do realistic zombie makeup again for a little while, but it was a heck of an experience, and we still giggle about it."

– Jeffrey Dean Morgan, Actor

Dancing dad. "It doesn't matter if I'm off the beat. It doesn't matter if I'm snapping to the rhythm. It doesn't matter if I look like a complete goon when I dance. It is my dance. It is my moment. It is mine. And dance I will. Try and stop me. You'll probably get kicked in the face."

— Dan Pearce, from "Single Dad Laughing"

Dad's love. "No one in this world can love a girl more than her father."

— Michael Ratnadeepak

Please don't text from school.

Son: Hey dad

Me: STOP TEXTING ME FROM SCHOOL YOU NEED TO PAY ATTENTION

Son: okay but the trailer for the new Call of Duty game just came out

Me: OMG SEND ME THE LINK

-- Unknown

My kids have two brains. "The first brain is the brain of a chimp and memory lasts only 20 seconds for instructions, directions, and chores around the house.

The second brain is the brain of an elephant. It doesn't forget a thing as long as they are promises of presents, toys, trips, and new video games, etc."

-- Anon.

White lies. "Fathers need to tell little white lies right from the start. They hand you something that looks like a cross between Gollum and a ball of bread dough, and you look at your wife and tell her it's the most beautiful thing you've ever seen."

-- Unknown

Sleep deprivation. "If anyone else deprived you of this much sleep, you'd have them up at The Hague for war crimes."

-- Tom Hardy, Actor

Should we have another baby? "Sometimes while he sleeps, we'll stand over his bed and admire this human we've brought into the world. In those moments it's hard not to want another child.

"But by morning he's awake. And we're sober. And to hell with that."

-- Unknown

Map folding. "If you ever want to torture my dad, tie him up and right in front of him, refold a map incorrectly."

— Cathy Ladman

Call the police. "My 5-year-old daughter lost her first tooth, and the tooth fairy came. The next day we were taking a video, and I panned down to her to record her impression, 'Did the tooth fairy come last night?'"

"And she goes, 'Someone was in our house?'"

"And I go, 'The tooth fairy was in our house!'"

She's like, 'Someone was in my room? While I was sleeping? And you guys are cool with this?'"

-- Bill Hader, Actor, Comedian

No appreciation. "Nobody appreciates Daddy. I'm talking about the real daddy that handles the [expletive] business. Nobody ever says, 'Hey, Daddy, thanks for knocking out this rent!' 'Hey, Daddy, I sure love this hot water!' 'Hey, Daddy, it's easy to read with all this light!'"

-- Chris Rock

Sharpshooters. "Boy diapers are different from girl diapers. We had the girl first. You get a very full sense of security when you change a girl diaper first, because it's never dangerous. There's nothing pointed at you. Oh. I - I learned the hard way. As soon as the boy diaper opens there's an infrared light on your head. Oh. You're target practice. You're - you're the target, that's what you are. They're good. They're sharpshooters. Twins are good because they compete with each other. 'Oh, nice shot! Nice shot! I didn't think you could reach him from there. Beautiful shot. All right. Watch this, I'll put his cigarette out now. Yeah.'"

-- Ray Romano

No procrastination.

Dad: You'll never amount to anything because you procrastinate.

Son: Oh yeah? Just you wait!

-- Anon.

Low blow. "Never raise your hand to your kids. It leaves your groin unprotected."

-- Red Buttons, Comedian

Forget about quiet conversations. "Having a conversation while having children is like trying to do your taxes in an inflatable jump house."

-- Unknown

Special dad. "Anyone can be a father, but it takes someone special to be a dad, and that's why I call you dad, because you are so special to me. You taught me the game and you taught me how to play it right."

— Wade Boggs, Professional baseball player and member of the champion Yankees, 1996 World Series

Just need to do it myself. "He tells me to park around the corner, and then he gets out and he walks to school. So, he did it to me the other day, after doing it about five times on the trot. So, I'm driving around, and he's just walking in his school, and I open the window said, 'Brooklyn! I love you!' And, you know, obviously it didn't go down very well."

– David Beckham

"**My youngest** is being tested for the gifted program but my other son thinks his toothbrush is haunted."

– Unknown.

Rules for dating my daughter.

1) Have a job
2) Understand I don't like you
3) I'm everywhere
4) You hurt her, and I will hurt you
5) Be home thirty minutes early
6) If you lie to me, I will know
7) She is my princess, not your conquest

8) I don't mind going back to prison

   -- Unknown

Warfare. "Raising kids is part joy and part guerrilla warfare."

   -- Ed Asner

More Guinness World Records. Locked down? Nothing to do? Consider fun attempts at breaking world records with your children.

(CAUTION: These may be highly dangerous. Please use them at your own risk with all proper safeguards before attempting any of these).

Please always check the current record at the time you might attempt any of these as these records change.

- This one may be a bit too much but FYI the largest collection of teddy bears in the world happens to be 20,367 bears and counting!

- Most Jell-O eaten using chopsticks in one minute. German André Ortolf ate 716 grams of Jell-O. That is a bit over seven full boxes of Jell-O.

- Jell-O eater, Mr. Ortolf, also has the record for the fastest time to put together a Mr. Potato Head toy -- while blindfolded. His record is 14.90 seconds.

- Tallest Sandcastle was built in Binz, Germany and it took almost a month to build. When it was finished, the sand structure measured 57.9 feet high (17.65 metres)!

- Most dogs walked in a conga line is held by 12-year-old German girl Alexa Lauenburger who had eight dogs walk together in a conga line.

Fatherhood. "To be a successful father, there's one absolute rule: when you have a kid, don't look at it for the first two years."

-- Ernest Hemingway

Walk through fire. "I'd walk through fire for my daughter. Well, not FIRE because it's dangerous. But a super humid room. But not too humid because of my hair."

-- Ryan Reynolds

Diapers. "Men should always change diapers. It's mentally cleansing. It's like washing dishes, but imagine if the dishes were your kids, so you really love the dishes."

-- Chris Martin

Invincible. "When I was a child, all problems had ended with a single word from my father. A smile from him was sunshine, his scowl a bolt of thunder. He was smart, and generous, and honorable without fail. He could exile a trespasser, check my math homework, and fix the leaky bathroom sink, all before dinner. For the longest time, I thought he was invincible and far above the petty problems that plagued normal people.

"And now he was gone."

— Rachel Vincent, from "Alpha"

Soccer game. "I was asked by a lady standing next to me which kid was mine. I told her, 'Do you see that kid whose scoring all the goals?'"

"Yes."

"Well, mine's the kid standing next to him pretending he's a dog."

    -- Unknown

Dad mends his daughter's broken heart. "At the ripe old age of 21, I was going through my first major breakup. I was a mess—I drove 24 hours home to 'heal.' Healing to me was treating my mom like a therapist, breaking into random tears, and slumming around the house. Eventually my poor mom had had enough and sent me over to visit my dad. My dad is a quiet man—he speaks very broken English and grew up in a world much different than mine. I speak broken Spanish, so we've always had a bit of a language barrier. Through tears, I explained what happened. To my surprise, my dad burst into laughter and told me that the guy was a jerk. He offered me a beer—the first beer we'd ever had together—and assured me that the first heartbreak is always the hardest. He was right."

    — Christina Nava

For the Father Who Has Everything by Team Golfwell

Thanks for letting me dream. "I've said it before, but it's absolutely true: My mother gave me my drive, but my father gave me my dreams. Thanks to him, I could see a future."

— Liza Minnelli

Have a boy under 7 years old? A father of boys under 7 years shares his observations and valuable advice,

"A king size waterbed holds enough water to fill a 2000 sq. ft. house, 4 inches deep."

"A 3-year-old boy's voice is louder than 200 adults in a crowded restaurant."

"Brake fluid mixed with Clorox makes smoke, and lots of it."

"Play dough and microwave should not be used in the same sentence."

"Super glue is forever."

"No matter how much Jell-O you put in a swimming pool you still can't walk on water."

"Pool filters do not like Jell-O."

"Garbage bags do not make good parachutes."

"Marbles in gas tanks make lots of noise when driving."

"You probably DO NOT want to know what that odor is."

"The fire department in Austin, Texas has a 5-minute response time."

"The spin cycle on the washing machine does not make earthworms dizzy."

"It will, however, make cats dizzy."

"Cats throw up twice their body weight when dizzy."

"Most men who read this will try mixing brake fluid with Clorox."

– Anon

Greatest gift. "My father gave me the greatest gift anyone could give another person, he believed in me."

— Jim Valvano

Late for school. "My kids would be late for school even if we lived inside the school."

-- Unknown.

3 am. "A baby crying is a weird thing. During the daytime you can listen to it and think that it's endearing and cute. At 3 a.m. it's like having the inside of your skull sandpapered by an angry Viking."

-- Matt Coyne

Dad makes the kids' lunches for school. "First week of school. Sandwiches cut in cute shapes, sliced fruit, and encouraging notes.

"Last week of school. Handful of croutons wrapped in foil."

-- Anon.

Being an actor. "Fatherhood is all about pretending neck ties are the best gifts you ever received."

-- Anon.

Pets.

Son: Dad, I have to tell you two things about my snake.

Dad: You have a snake?

Son: Right. And the second thing is it's missing from my room.

-- Anon.

A man's daughter. "A man's daughter is his heart. Just with feet, walking out in the world."

— Mat Johnson, Author

Beard. "My 4-year-old saw my razor on the bathroom counter and asked me what it was. So, I told him it's Mommies and she uses it to shave her really thick curly beard.

"I can't wait for him to tell all his friends."

-- Anon.

Eloquence of example. "I watched a small man with thick calluses on both hands work 15 and 16 hours a day. I saw him once literally bleed from the bottoms of his feet, a man who came here uneducated, alone, unable to speak the language, who taught me all I needed to know about faith and hard work by the simple eloquence of his example."

--Mario Cuomo, former New York governor

Pizza. "Tonight my 4-year-old told me that I made the best pizza he's ever had.

"So, if you think I'm going to take credit for a cheap supermarket owned brand frozen pizza you are absolutely correct."

-- Unknown

Dad says goodnight. It's bedtime.

Me: "Goodnight kids."

Kids: "Goodnight dad."

Me: "Goodnight monster that eats children who are bad."

Mom: (Through the intercom) "GOODNIGHT!"

On the serious side. "I learned the hard way. I learned what not to do."

– New York City Mayor Bill de Blasio, talking about what he learned from his father who unfortunately was an alcoholic who killed himself when former Mayor Bill de Blasio was 18.

Want to teach your kids how to sell? Some say the better salesperson you are the better you will deal with life. Most of us (unless you're Royalty?) sooner or later must sell our views in some way or another. For the fun of it, here is an ingenious "salesperson game" kids seem to enjoy that might expand their thinking.

You start this game by trying to sell your children something they don't want or need. For example, try to sell them a broken umbrella, or a broken shoelace, or last year's wall calendar, or a dead battery, or a shoe or a sock with a hole in it, etc.

After you show them how to sell it ask them to try to sell things they don't want or need to you. Your children may surprise you to show how creative and persuasive they can be.

If they can't come up with crazy things to sell, a list follows with items to sell, and feel free to come up with your own – the funnier the better! They could try to sell you,

- Left-handed baseball glove
- A flyswatter with a hole in it
- A paper cup with a hole in the bottom
- A sock with a hole in the toe
- A jump rope with a broken rope
- A staircase that goes nowhere
- Diet water
- A tennis racquet with no strings
- A rubber ball that doesn't bounce,
- A Bulgarian dictionary, etc.

Heart of a Father. "The heart of a father is the masterpiece of nature."

— Prevost Abbe, from "Manon Lescaut"

Teach a kid to fish. "Give a kid a fish, and he'll ask for chicken nuggets."

"Teach a kid to fish, and he'll ask for chicken nuggets."

– Anon.

Understanding it. "Anyone who tells you fatherhood is the greatest thing that can happen to you, they are understanding it."

— Mike Myers

Robot car. Joe bought a voice automated robot car that does anything he tells it to do correctly without any error.

Joe was very proud of what the car could do, and the car didn't make any mistakes.

One day, Joe was home, and his wife told him to tell the car to go and pick up the children from school. She was tired.

Joe agreed and said to the car: "Car, go and bring my children from school."

The car took off but didn't return as it usually does.

Joe and his wife thought something must be wrong and both became concerned after several hours passed.

Joe was ready to call the police when he and his wife saw the robot car approaching overloaded with children.

The car parked right in front of them and announced, "These are your children, sir."

Seated in the car were the neighbor's children, the schoolteacher's children, his wife's best friend's children, and his sister-in-law's children.

Joe's wife said, "Joe! Don't tell me all these are your children!"

Joe replied, "Can you first tell me why our children are not in the car?"

Guns don't kill people. Dads with pretty daughters kill people.

    -- Unknown

Role reversal. The nomadic Central African tribe known as the Aka Pygmy tribe are hunters and gatherers. Only the women can be the hunters, and the men can stay and mind the children.

Professor Barry Hewlett, an American anthropologist, reports that according to the data he began collecting more than two decades ago, Aka Pygmy fathers are within reach of their infants 47% of the time - that's apparently more than fathers in any other cultural group on the planet, which is why Fathers Direct has decided to dub the Aka Pygmy dads as "the best dads in the world". [26]

The amazing tribe has a culture where the male and female roles are virtually interchangeable. While the women hunt, the men mind the children; while the men cook, the women decide where to set up the next camp. And vice versa: and it's in this vice versa, says Hewlett, that the important message lies. "There is a sexual division of labour in the Aka community - women, for example, are the primary caregivers," he says. "But and this is crucial, there's a level of flexibility that's virtually unknown in our society. Aka fathers will slip into roles usually occupied by mothers without a second thought and without, more importantly, any loss of status - there's no stigma involved in the different jobs." are the primary caregivers," he says.

"The point about the Aka," says Hewlett, "is that the active role the fathers have is simply one facet of their entire approach to life, and it's that approach as much as anything that we can learn from. One thing that's crucial in the raising of the young is the importance placed on physical closeness: at around three months, a baby is in almost constant physical contact with either one of her parents or with another person. There's no such thing as a cot in an Aka camp because it's unheard of for a couple to ever leave their baby lying unattended - babies are held all the time." [27]

Repeating yourself. "Parents say a lot of things over and over. For example, I just said 'Please don't pull Daddy's pants down in public.' for the 200th time."

-- Unknown

Turning into your dad? Lately, all my friends are worried that they're turning into their fathers. I'm worried that I'm not.

-- Dan Zevin

Six other societies where dads are secondary. The ladies run these modern-day societies. [28]

1) Near the border of Tibet in the Yunnan and Sichuan provinces, the Mosuo are perhaps the most famous matrilineal society

(matrilineal means that all property, etc. goes through the female line). The Mosuo live with extended family in large households; and the head of each family is the oldest woman and property is passed down along the women's relatives. The women primarily handle business. They also have "walking marriages" and women choose the dad by walking to the man's home, sleeping there, and then returning to her home. The couples don't live together. In some cases, the father's identity is not even known. The children stay with mom.

2) The Minangkabau people (and there are 4 million of them) are in West Sumatra, Indonesia, and are the largest known matrilineal society. Tribal law requires all clan property to be held and bequeathed from mother to daughter as they believe the mother to be the most important person in society. However, the clan chief is male. But and as you might have guessed, women have the absolute right to select the clan chief and remove him from office if he fails his duties.

3) The Akan people in Ghana also have a society built around women. Property is also passed through the female line. The man is expected to not only support his own family, but those of his female relatives. So, it makes you appreciate things a bit more especially if you take up living with the Akan people.

4) The Bribri are roughly 13,000 people living in the Talamanca canton in the Limón province of Costa Rica who also have a matrilineal society. The Bribri live in clans and each clan is made

up of extended family in accordance with the line determined through the mother/females. Women are the only ones who traditionally can inherit land. The old song, "Mother-in-Law" which was a big hit in 1961 sung by Ernie Doe, isn't very popular there.

5) The Garo people in North-East India are governed by men but according to their laws, pall property must pass from mother to daughter who is typically the youngest daughter. Marriages are also arranged according to Garo tradition, where the groom-to-be is expected to run away from a proposal of marriage, and the bride-to-be's family captures and brings him to his potential bride's village. After the marriage ceremony, the husband lives in his wife's house but if the marriage doesn't work, they both go their separate ways as marriage is not a binding contract.

It seems if you are the "chosen one" and you want to stay single, etc., you need to train very hard to be quick on your feet to avoid being captured. If you do avoid capture or if disagreement develops, the would-be bride's family chooses another possible husband, and so on.

6) Be careful whose garden you work on. The Nagovisi people live in South Bougainville, and that is an island west of New Guinea. The women are the leaders and take pride in working their lands. When it comes to marriage, the Nagovisi woman holds gardening and sex of equal importance. If a couple is seen together and sleeps

together, and if the man regularly assists the woman with her garden, for all purposes they are considered married. [29]

Being a dad. "Being a dad means always being a shoulder to cry on.

And wipe your nose on.

And spit up on.

I'm basically just a human napkin."

– Unknown.

Name game. My 4-year-old, "Hi, Daddy Daddy bo fatty!"

(Just want to give my special thanks to whoever taught him that name game banana song thing.)

– Unknown

These things made my 2-year-old cry this week.

- I wouldn't let the dog drive him to daycare.

- The bath was "too wet."

- He wants syrup for breakfast – just syrup.

- His sister keeps looking at him.

- He wants shoes just like his friend Frankie (there is no Frankie).

-- Anon.

More world records to consider breaking.

(CAUTION: Again, these may be highly dangerous to try and use them at your own risk with all proper safeguards).

Again, please always check the current record at the time you might attempt any of these as these records change.

- The Fastest Half-Marathon While Pushing a Stroller. Canadian dad Callum Neff ran a half-marathon in 1 hour, 11 minutes, and 27 seconds, pushing his 11-month-old daughter, Holland.

- Recently, in September 2021, David Rush enlisted the help of his 5-year-old son to break a Guinness World Record for the fastest 10-meter (32.8 feet) shuttle run while pushing a stroller. The record requires his son be at least 44 pounds and he broke the 15-second record by doing the run in 10.04 seconds.

- David Rush, who has broken more than 200 Guinness records to promote STEM education, said the stroller run record had been on his radar for a couple of years, but he had to wait for his son to meet the minimum weight requirement of 44 pounds.

- Youngest DJ. Archie Norbury, known as DJ Archie, holds the record for the world's youngest DJ when he performed at Bungalow in Hong Kong. He was 4 years old.

- Youngest female to climb Mount Kilimanjaro is Montannah Kenney when she was 7 years old and accompanied by her mother. Mt Kilimanjaro has a height of 19,341 feet. She did it be closer to her father in heaven, who had died five years earlier.

- The record for the longest hair for a teenager is Indian Nilanshi Patel who at 17, hadn't gotten her hair cut since the age of 6. Here hair measured a length of 5 feet 7 inches (170.5 cm) in 2018. FYI the adult record-holder Xie Qiuping's whose hair is 18 feet long.

A bright future. My two-year-old only cares about himself, cries when he doesn't get his way, and lies constantly. Looks like he's going to be a great politician.

-- Anon.

Dad's rules. My sisters and I can still recite Dad's grilling rules:

Rule No. 1: Dad is in charge.

Rule No. 2: Repeat Rule No. 1.

-- Connie Schultz

Viewpoint change.

Dad before he had kids, "I won't ever lie to my children."

Dad after kids, "Eating candy after dinner will make you poop spiders."

-- Unknown.

Being humble. "It isn't hard to be humble when your 6-year-old tells you, "You have a big fat belly like Daddy Pig."

-- Anon.

Street performer. "When I was a year old, I had to have a foot amputated due to medical reasons. A few weeks after I had the amputation, my parents were pushing me around in a stroller at a street festival in Miami and I was like waving and chewing on my good leg and foot and a street performer came up to us and looked at me and said, 'Oh I bet that tastes gooood.'

"My dad pulled up the blanket to show a stump and huge scar on my other leg and said, 'Yeah, look what she did to the other one.'

"I was told the poor street performer was terrified and left very quickly."

-- Natalie

Unexplained rash. "I got some kind of allergic reaction, and my face is breaking out in a horrible rash and my mom is freaking out and wants to take me to the ER and my dad was like, 'Let's not make any rash decisions' and we high-fived and now my mom is yelling at us."

-- Anon.

Example. "I talk and talk and talk, and I haven't taught people in 50 years what my father taught by example in one week."

-- Maria Cuomo Cole

Why?

"**Four-year-old**: 'Tell me a scary story!'

Me: 'One-time little people popped out of your mom, and they never stopped asking questions.'

Four -year-old: 'Why?'"

-- Anon

The older I get. "The older I get the more I can see how much he loved my mother and my brother and me.

"And he did the best that he could, and I only hope when I have my own family, that every day I see a little more of my father in me."

— Keith Urban

"I'm coming!" I know that if my mom fell and screamed for help, my dad would jump right up to rescue her as soon as it was halftime.

– Bruce Cameron. Author, columnist, and humorist

Fatherhood didn't just happen to me. I am deliberately living it, re-imagining it, and rediscovering it every day. It is as beautiful as I make it, just like anything else in life.

– Hrithik Roshan, Actor

Loved. "My father would lift me high

And dance with my mother and me and then

Spin me around til I fell asleep.

Then up the stairs he would carry me

And I knew for sure I was loved."

— Luther Vandross

Father's Day gift. "The nicest Father's Day surprise of all for Dad would be if you handed him a box, and he unwrapped it, and there, inside, sitting on a bed of folded tissue, was the pair of his undershorts that somebody threw away six months ago (without asking Dad) because they had reached the stage where they were 3 percent undershorts and 97 percent holes.

"Dad misses those undershorts. They were his Faithful Undershorts Companion."

— Dave Barry

Alzheimer's. "I love my dad, because even though he has Alzheimer's, he remembers the important things. He can't remember my name, but last week he told me exactly how much money I owe him."

-- Thyra Lees-Smith

Tearing up the grass? "My father used to play with my brother and me in the yard. Mother would come out and say, 'You're tearing up the grass.'

'We're not raising grass' Dad would reply. 'We're raising boys.'"

-- Harmon Killebrew.

Age doesn't matter. "No matter how old we are, we still need our dads, and wonder how we'll get by without them."

– Jennifer Williamson

Tribe. "I asked my dad for a BB gun, but he said we were a tribe of worriers, not warriors."

-- Hilary Price

Diapers. "Spread the diaper in the position of the diamond with you at-bat. Then, fold second base down to home and set the baby on the pitcher's mound. Put first base and third together, bring up home plate and pin the three together. Of course, in case of rain, you gotta call the game and start all over again."

-- Jimmy Piersall

What you do carries on. "No matter where I am, your spirit will be beside me. For I know that no matter what, you will always be with me."

– Tram-Tiara T. von Reichenbach

We hope you enjoyed our book!

If you liked our book, we would sincerely appreciate your taking a few moments to leave a brief review.

Thank you again very much!

TeamGolfwell and Bruce Miller

About the authors

Bruce Miller. Lawyer, businessman, world traveler, golf enthusiast, and Golf Rules Official, actor, shrewd gambler, whiskey connoisseur, and author of over 35 books, a few being Amazon bestsellers, spends his days writing, studying, and constantly learning of the astounding, unexpected, and amazing events happening in the world today while exploring the brighter side of life. He is a member of Team Golfwell, Authors, and Publishers.

TeamGolfwell are bestselling authors and founders of the very popular 200,000+ member Facebook Group "Golf Jokes and Stories." Their books have sold thousands of copies including several #1 bestsellers in Golf Coaching, Sports humor, and other categories.

We Want to Hear from You!

"There usually is a way to do things better and there is opportunity when you find it." - Thomas Edison

We love to hear your thoughts and suggestions on anything and please feel free to contact us at Bruce@TeamGolfwell.com

Other Books by Team Golfwell and Bruce Miller

Brilliant Screen-Free Stuff to Do with Kids: A Handy Reference for Parents & Grandparents!

For the Golfer Who Has Everything: A Funny Golf Book

Dragonflies: A Novel Based on What Men Think of Women

The Funniest Quotations to Brighten Every Day: Brilliant, Inspiring, and Hilarious Thoughts from Great Minds

Jokes for Very Funny Kids (Big & Little): A Treasury of Funny Jokes and Riddles Ages 9 - 12 and Up

And more here and here.

For the Father Who Has Everything by Team Golfwell

Index to paragraphs

Who needs who the most? 1

Make your life easier 1

"Always knew that…" 1

Raising children. 2

"Watch your ass." 2

Best friend 2

Father suddenly becomes a genius. 2

A daughter's gift – I think? 3

Try..3

"I've lost my dad" 3

Bring her home on time. 4

Hide and seek. 4

"Give a dad a fish 4

What's a perfect dad?...4

Confident and Confidential 6

You want a piece of me?..6

Wrong answer! 7

For the Father Who Has Everything by Team Golfwell

Son runs into dad's ghost in a video game. 7

Dad jokes 8

Father and daughter climb Mt. Everest. 9

Show don't tell. 9

Raising daughters. 9

Things my dad would not say. 9

Sex talk from dad 10

Cycle 10

Get a lock. 10

A great man died today. 11

The difference between a son and a daughter. 12

Friend and role model. 12

Don't tell me about numbers! 12

Say what? 13

Slip of the tongue. 13

Learn a trade. 14

Pat of butter. 14

Who started Father's Day? 15

Let's go drinking 15

For the Father Who Has Everything by Team Golfwell

The cat's out of the bag. 15

Do you want to discover your children's general knowledge? 16

Al Unser 17

Learning the order of numbers 17

Dad? 18

Don't clap. 18

Shooting beavers. 18

Walks it instead of talks it 19

Great fathers 19

Father's Day gift from a daughter 20

Doesn't matter 20

Embarrassed dad! 20

Fishing and shopping 21

A child's laugh 21

A few dad jokes. 21

Taller 23

Father-daughter one-handed crack an egg world record 23

No equal 24

Stand by me 24

For the Father Who Has Everything by Team Golfwell

Bored with the kids at home? 24

Who's the boss? 26

Father's Day tradition. 27

Don't need drugs. 27

Dad is into Peppa pig. 28

Frat house. 28

Slip of the tongue. 28

It's not too late! 29

Disappointing looks. 29

Dad is real 29

Support 30

God took the strength of a mountain and 30

New baby on the way? 31

Dad's advice 31

What's hard about being a dad? 32

What happens at 12 weeks after being born? 32

They may not say it 32

Some dad jokes you may not have heard before. 32

Indescribable 34

For the Father Who Has Everything by Team Golfwell

85-year-old dad sets Mount Kilimanjaro climb record 34

War? 35

Different father? 35

"I do like a proper hug and snuggle 36

A father called his five small children together 36

Want an ambitious daughter? 36

Where does the moon go? 37

Dads are ordinary men 37

Treat them like sons 37

How much? 37

Roses are tough, ... 38

Move over 38

Hint, Hint 38

Thank you from your daughter 39

How true 39

Happy (technical) Father's Day! 40

Want lots of kids? 40

Drive thru 41

Good father 41

For the Father Who Has Everything by Team Golfwell

Storyteller. 41

What we become 43

The real thrill 43

Marathon running 43

It's bedtime 44

Living up to dad 44

Sissy Magazine? 44

Teaching sons. 45

Rainy day stuff to do with small kids 45

Can't help but do this 46

Daddy issues? Not my daughter 46

Who? 46

What is a dad? 47

Stories about dads 47

Benefits. 49

Riding on your shoulders 49

On dad's shoulders 49

Best years 50

Smart dad! 50

For the Father Who Has Everything by Team Golfwell

Love 50

Single dads..50

Titles 51

Got to know dad. 51

Connection...51

How fathers were created. 51

Drinking fountain fact..53

Daughters growing up. 53

How many fathers and sons have been US Presidents? 54

Double standard...54

Beyond words...54

Can a dad be pregnant?..54

Tough taking the temperature..55

Why is dad the enemy? 55

Need money?..55

Pretending?...56

A picture is worth a thousand words. 56

Putting kids to bed is easy..56

Unseen tears. 57

For the Father Who Has Everything by Team Golfwell

Losing weight. 57

Or in other words. 57

Diaper race! 58

Creation 58

Thank you, dad, from your daughter 58

Dancing dads 58

Great father 59

Plane rides 59

Fathers understand this 59

Knowledge acquired too late 59

Example 60

How do you figure? 60

"Everybody thinks their dad's jokes are corny. 61

First-time dad. 61

This is all you have to do 61

The poorest dad 61

The richest dad 62

Most kids. 62

Role model 62

Am I teaching her about the future? ... 63

A bit confused? ... 63

Delayed appreciation for dad. ... 64

The one and only Rodney Dangerfield… ... 64

Melts away. ... 65

Security cameras catch dad's ghost. ... 65

"If you're my father and if you love me…". ... 66

Just kidding! ... 67

Show him the world. ... 67

What a father does ... 68

How to be cool ... 68

Dad could do that. ... 69

I'm thinking… ... 69

Great moments. ... 70

Dancing dad. ... 70

Dad's love. ... 71

Please don't text from school. ... 71

My kids have two brains. ... 71

White lies. ... 72

For the Father Who Has Everything by Team Golfwell

Sleep deprivation 72

Should we have another baby? 72

Map folding 73

Call the police. 73

No appreciation 74

Sharpshooters. 74

No procrastination 74

Low blow 75

Forget about quiet conversations. 75

Special dad 75

Just need to do it myself. 76

"My youngest 76

Rules for dating my daughter. 76

Warfare 77

More Guinness World Records 77

Fatherhood 78

Walk through fire 79

Diapers 79

Invincible 79

For the Father Who Has Everything by Team Golfwell

Soccer game. 80

Dad mends his daughter's broken heart. 80

Thanks for letting me dream 81

Have a boy under 7 years old? 81

Greatest gift. 82

Late for school 83

3 am. 83

Dad makes the kids' lunches for school 83

Being an actor 83

Pets 84

A man's daughter 84

Beard 84

Eloquence of example. 85

Pizza 85

Dad says goodnight 85

On the serious side 86

Want to teach your kids how to sell? 86

Heart of a Father. 87

Teach a kid to fish 88

For the Father Who Has Everything by Team Golfwell

Understanding it 88

Robot car 88

Guns don't kill people 89

Role reversal. 90

Repeating yourself. 91

Turning into your dad? 91

Six other societies where dads are secondary. 91

Being a dad 94

Name game 94

These things made my 2-year-old cry this week. 94

More world records to consider breaking 95

A bright future. 97

Dad's rules 97

Viewpoint change 97

Being humble 98

Street performer. 98

Unexplained rash 99

Example 99

Why? 99

For the Father Who Has Everything by Team Golfwell

The older I get 100

"I'm coming!" 100

Fatherhood didn't just happen to me 100

Loved. 100

Father's Day gift 101

Alzheimer's 101

Tearing up the grass? 102

Age doesn't matter 102

Tribe 102

Diapers 103

What you do carries on 103

We hope you enjoyed our book! 104

About the authors 104

We Want to Hear from You! 105

Other Books by Team Golfwell and Bruce Miller 106

References

[1] Motherly, https://www.mother.ly/life/health-wellness/the-science-benefits-of-roughhousing-with-your-kids-that-will-make-you-less-anxious/
[2] Ibid.
[3] Yahoo news, Motoramic, https://sg.news.yahoo.com/blogs/motoramic/teenage-son-discovers-his-deceased-father-s-ghost-car-in-xbox-rally-game-154558866.html
[4] Ibid.
[5] Guinness World Records, https://www.guinnessworldrecords.com/news/2018/6/fathers-day-7-awesome-dads-who-are-also-record-holders-529467
[6] Wikipedia, https://en.wikipedia.org/wiki/Sonora_Smart_Dodd
[7] Supra, https://www.guinnessworldrecords.com/news/2018/6/fathers-day-7-awesome-dads-who-are-also-record-holders-529467
[8] World Records to you can attempt at home, https://www.cuckooland.com/blog/world-records-you-can-attempt-at-home-with-your-children
[9] Guinness World Records, https://www.guinnessworldrecords.com/world-records/oldest-father-
[10] Wikipedia, https://en.wikipedia.org/wiki/Ramjit_Raghav#
[11] Ibid.
[12] Proceedings at the National Academy of Sciences of the United States, https://www.pnas.org/content/108/39/16194
[13] Ibid.

[14] Supra, https://www.guinnessworldrecords.com/news/2018/6/fathers-day-7-awesome-dads-who-are-also-record-holders-529467

[15] Ibid.

[16] CTV News, https://www.ctvnews.ca/health/dads-who-do-household-chores-more-likely-to-have-ambitious-daughters-study-1.1842286#

[17] Guinness Book of World Records, https://web.archive.org/web/20100313155522/http://www.guinnessworldrecords.com/news/2008/03/080303.aspx

[18] Ibid.

[19] Guinness World Records, https://www.guinnessworldrecords.com/world-records/fastest-marathon-run-by-parent-and-child

[20] Wikipedia, https://en.wikipedia.org/wiki/Drinking_fountain

[21] The Conversation, https://theconversation.com/curious-kids-is-it-true-that-male-seahorses-give-birth-92843

[22] NCBI, https://www.ncbi.nlm.nih.gov/pmc/articles/PMC4302344/

[23] Wikipedia, https://en.wikipedia.org/wiki/Feodor_Vassilyev

[24] Mirror, UK, https://www.mirror.co.uk/news/us-news/woman-spots-ghost-father-visiting-22592234

[25] Human Performance Resources, https://www.hprc-online.org/social-fitness/family-optimization/coaching-your-kids-emotions

[26] The Guardian, https://www.theguardian.com/society/2005/jun/15/childrensservices.familyandrelationships

[27] Ibid.

[28] Mentalfloss, https://www.mentalfloss.com/article/31274/6-modern-societies-where-women-literally-rule

[29] Ibid.

www.ingramcontent.com/pod-product-compliance
Lightning Source LLC
Chambersburg PA
CBHW021427070526
44577CB00001B/104